The Slightly Larger Book of

Despair

by

Arnie Claggerhaus

Founder of the Arnie Claggerhaus
University
Motto: A Degree of your choice by return.
Send an s.a.e!

Inventor of the desperation-enhancing
silent yodelling technique, in which breath
is sucked backwards through the larynx
while standing in an anacoustic chamber!

Discoverer of the Universal Law of
Desperation!

'Despair can work miracles!'

Published by Bewildered Books!

Produced by Lateral Marketing Consultants!
Bewildered Books is an imprint of
The Bewildered Publishing Company Ltd!

The Slightly Larger Book of Despair!
© 2000 John Wilson!
Another genuine First Edition!

ISBN 1-903247-01-2

Editor's statement

This book is typeset in 14 point Black Forest Gateau Roman from the original manuscript complete with Editorial notes in the hope that …

(*Ed.* Hold it right there! I told you not to use the '**H**' word! *AC*!)

(*Arnie*. Sorry, it just slipped out. I'll start again. *Ed.*)

Editor's statement

This book is typeset in 14 point Black Forest Gateau Roman from the original manuscript complete with Editorial notes. This is to help American literary institutions, desperate to acquire an insight into an author's mind via annotated manuscripts, to pay us a large sum of money for the printout. We are also including, for the same reason, excerpts from letters and emails received by the author during his research together with transcripts of security tapes recently released to the public under the Dissemination of Misleading Information Act.

Note from the Commercial Director of Bewildered Books

Inside this book we mention the trade names Ann Summers, Penguin Books, Microsoft, Kelloggs, Jack Barclays, Oddbins and Millets and the Welsh county of Ceredigion! Would the chairmen of these organisations please send a suitably large cheque to ensure editorial independence.

For more copies of this book, email: sales@bewildered.co.uk
Reader comments, email: readers@bewildered.co.uk
Web site: http://www.bewildered.co.uk
or fax: 01974 298 708

The Slightly Larger Book of
Despair

by
Arnie Claggerhaus

A Bewildered Books production

To the reader

Call me over-sensitive. Call me envious, jealous, vitriolic … call me what you like. But I cannot believe he's done it again, not after my cogent rebuttal of his beastly ideas.

Who has done what again, I hear you cry … and why are you so upset?

The antipodean guru, is who I mean. I refuse to use his name, but he is the same chap who deluged an already somnolent world with all this nonsense about keeping calm. I honestly thought my world best seller *The Slightly Larger Book of Panic* would have seen the man off, in no uncertain terms. But here he comes again with his unctuous and life-threatening advice. *The Little Book of Hope*, indeed!

(*Arnie*. The 'H' word ?? *Ed.*)

(*Ed*. It's okay if *I* use it. I'm the author and a Fellow of the World Institution of Lexical Philologists. I know how far I can go in breaking the rules. *AC.*)

… where was I? Oh yes … Under normal circumstances, I would have ignored his facile homilies, but my recent discovery of an entirely

4

new phobia has compelled me to react. I refer to *phobiophobia*, of which more later.

Suffice it to say in this brief but powerfully succinct introduction that if anything is more inhibiting to human survival than 'calm' it has to be 'hope'.

I put it to you, dear reader, in terms that a simpleton can understand. Each week in our beloved nation* 20,000,000 citizens pay £1 or more into the National Lottery because they hope they might win the jackpot.

Now, ask yourself, how many do win?

Still unconvinced? Then try this …

In 1998, 167 American men and women were put to death by electrocution, lethal injection, hanging and the bullet. They had between them spent thousands of years on Death Row, each hoping for a reprieve. Fat chance!

In this slightly larger book, I will convince you that despair, not hope, is the best way forward. If you don't believe me, then you cannot afford not to continue reading.

This book might save your sanity or your life. **It might even resurrect you, as it did me!**

A. Clopprbrz

Claggerhaus is not, strictly speaking, a British name. I understand it has its origins in the foothills of Scandinavia, where my ancestors kept a 'clagger' (rhymes with shagger) 'haus' (rhymes with house) to supply the testicular needs of itinerant bankers who were secretly financing the fledgling Hauptklein empire. You have not heard of the Hauptklein empire, because the bankers shagged themselves to a standstill before it got off the ground. You got the Weimar Republic instead. Meanwhile, my forefathers settled in Bedford and founded the nation's brick industry, the link here being that a claggerhaus was built with mud or clay, and the same is true of millions of post-Industrial-Revolution British homes. That was many, many years ago, so I believe I can claim to be as British as anyone; as British, possibly, as Her Majesty the Queen and Prince Philip, whose ethnicities are German and Greek, respectively.

(*Arnie*. I am <u>really</u> having a problem with this. As one who rejoiced at the recent visit of Her Majesty the Queen to Sydney, I find your work to date patronising, discursive and exclamatory, not to mention seditious. My contacts in MI5 take any reference to the Royal family and their ethnicities extremely seriously. Is there any way you can sort this, before things get out of hand? *Ed*.)

(*Ed*. There is one way, but you're not going to like it. You're fired! I didn't spend half my life in an iron lung to …)

(*Reader*. See Professor Claggerhaus's first book, *The Slightly Larger Book of Panic*, for an explanation of his 'iron lung' reference. *Ed.*)

(… to listen to this kind of rubbish. I'll find myself an editor with the intellectual brain power to keep up with me. *AC.*)

(*Arnie*. You pompous bastard! And, just for the record: keeping up with you is not a problem. A one-legged child on a fucking hobby horse could keep up with you. *Ed.*)

(*Ed.* Aha! I get it! You have just given your pathetic little game away. You aren't a real book editor, at all, are you? *AC.*)

(*Arnie*. And just what pathetic little game might that be? *Ed.*)

(*Ed.* It was Sydney and the Anglo-Saxon-expletive hobby horse references. Only an Australian could think up such an atrocious and vulgar metaphor and use so many exclamation marks. I have just run your communications through a quantum syllabic sequence analyser. Stand up Paul Wilson, author of appalling little books and would-be saboteur of my slightly larger books … *AC.*)

(*Arnie*. You pompous pommy bastard! I hope these infernal manuscript notes ruin your bloody writing!! *ex-Ed.*)

Despair and hope: the dichotomy

If you are fortunate enough to have already absorbed the wisdom contained in my *Slightly Larger Book of Panic*, you are well prepared for what follows, and you will know that the first thing we have to deal with is the nature of despair and its relationship with its *alter nuomo* (*sic*), hope.

Philologists will be the first to admit that if a word exists in a language there's a very good reason. In that context, despair is intimately connected to hope through the common Latin stem, *spero*, as in *spero* = hope and *despero* = no hope.

The same connections existed in ancient Greece, as in σπερο = hope and δεσπερο = no hope; not to mention the Assyrian ▲◻＊◻◻ = hope and ＊＊▲◻＊◻◻ = no hope, symbols carved on a rock near the ancient city of Petra and discovered by the intrepid and scandalously neglected British explorer and the founder of modern archaeology, Sir Henry Austin Layard, who discovered the lost city of Nineveh.

We can deduce from this that ancient and literate peoples knew all about hope and despair and saw them as one philological continuum, not the two aspirational extremes conjured up by modern society.

Does the difference in our approach matter? Does it make any difference?

Of course it does. Can anyone imagine Alexander the Great looking up at the pass at the Hindu Kush and telling his hand-picked men: 'Gee, fellahs, I hope we can get up there before the Persians spot us'?

Of course not! He stood in front of his men and said: 'Last one up is a flaying job'.

Desperation, not hope, got them up that hill, at night, in full armour and only a castrated shepherd to guide them.

Anyone needing further proof should consider the post-Alexandrian statements: 'While there's life there's hope' and 'It's hopeless'.

These two contradictory notions co-exist happily in our confused and confusing lexicon of expressions. Those who utter them do so in tones that brook no argument from the hapless recipient who, faced with an apparently insoluble problem, is obliged to accept advice from the first person who comes along.

[The postman has just arrived, and under the terms of my contract I am obliged to make a note of this interruption. I wonder what that strange envelope is, with the foreign stamp.]

Professor A. Claggerhaus Esq
c/o Bewildered Books
Ceredigion, Wales

Dear Professor Claggerhaus

I have seen your compelling advertisement in today's Evening Standard for the position of freelance Editor for your new book, The Slightly Larger Book of Despair, and I believe I am admirably well qualified to undertake such a pleasant task.

I am holding five first class honours degrees and three doctorates from the University of Darjeeling and am a member of the Baswami Ghat body fencing team.

Perhaps a word of explanation of the latter pursuit is in order.

Many years ago, a travelling Frenchman left behind in our village a copy of the world famous book, The Three Musketeers. This was presented to our guru with all due pomp and ceremony, and he undertook a momentous critique of the work. In doing so, he is revealing a great anomaly: not once in all its eight thousand five hundred and thirty-two pages is even one of the three eponymous musketeering heroes firing a musket. On the contrary, as we might say. Their chosen method of personal armament is the rapier.

It was in an atmosphere of hushed silence among his people that the village guru delivered this critical analysis, and the next few days were spent drafting a letter to the Editor of The Times of London using the good offices of my own great-great-great-great-grandfather, who was the village scribe, and so you are seeing that the business of editing is within my blood and genomes.

Meanwhile the inventive but poverty stricken and ferrously-challenged villagers adapted the art of fencing to that of the also much-needed act of procreation, and thus the symbolic art of body fencing was created, using matched pairs of male and female protagonists.

By these means, our tiny population survived earthquake, fire, pestilence, flood, cyclone and the egress of the East India company from our shores.

Leaving me to remain,

Yours, Sir, In Hope.

Doctor Rambal Phal (Graduate and Fellow of the University of Darjeeling)

———————

[The cheek of the man! I'll soon sort him out ...]

Doctor Rambal Phal
c/o District Sub-Post Office
Ashokaga
Either India or Pakistan

Dear Doctor Rambal Phal

Thank you so much for writing to apply for the position of Editor.

I am delighted to tell you that you have not been selected for an interview with all travelling expenses paid and a fortnight's stay at the Dorchester Hotel in Park Lane with an ex-Miss World contestant as your constant companion.

Had you been successful in your application, your salary would have been £50,000 per annum with six months paid leave, unlimited medical expenses and your choice of company car from the world famous Jack Barclay showrooms in Mayfair.

Having such a total idiot as yourself not working for my company is one of the continuing pleasures of an otherwise frustrating life.

Yours sincerely
Arnie Claggerhaus (DSc and Bar)

[Stick that up your qualifications, Dr Dr Dr Phal!]

The failure of hope

Show me the man or woman who, when presented with a solution to his problem, says 'Let's hope it works', and I'll show you a loser.

Hope is such a dangerous and pernicious strategy that I am now about to do the one thing I promised myself not to do: I am going to trash The Little Book of Hope as written by my ex-editor.

As it happens, I need travel no further than Page 3 to do this. (If you are stupid enough to own a copy, you'll note that the pages are not numbered. This is a deliberate ploy to make criticism difficult.)

There, in purple Monotype Phaistos, is the give-away: *'Let this book fall open to any page for the suggestion that will work best for you at this moment.'*

Fair enough, you might say.

The trouble is, the book will not fall open to any page. No matter how many times you drop it from whatever distance, it remains firmly and hopelessly closed.

At first, I thought it might be me, doing it wrongly. So I dropped it from varying heights and onto a variety of different floor coverings and other substances, such as plywood, grass, Welsh slate and Kellogg's Branflakes. I even considered sheep shit. It's lambing time at the moment, and there's a lot around, but you have to look ahead in my game, and I didn't fancy picking it up again.

I quickly understood why the book would not open: it is very small indeed and bound by a method called 'perfect', which means gluing the pages together down the spine. This makes it very stiff. If you drop it, it bounces and hops, but it does not open.

In desperation I tried another technique: I tried to flush it down the lavatory bowl. Needless to say, it refused to pass round the U-bend. However (and this exemplifies my entire philosophy regarding the superior power of despair), it eventually began to fall apart.

Guess which page floated to the top! In the certainty that a few words of quotation will not render me liable for copyright payment, I quote:

TAKE PLEASURE IN AN EMPTY BOWL
There's an old Zen saying: 'Only an empty bowl can be filled'. It means that the moment you think you have nothing left is the moment when growth and progress become inevitable. Every time you see an empty bowl, think of the potential.

Come on, fellahs! No one can fill an empty bowl, no matter how many tonnes of curry you had the night before. And, despite our best efforts, half the population of the world doesn't even have a lavatory bowl, never mind an empty one.

It's not Hope that inspires people to drive aid lorries to Kosovo or Mozambique: it's Desperation.

It's not Hope that will stop that trillion-tonne asteroid smashing our world to bits: it will be the desperate efforts of scientists and technologists, struggling on diminishing budgets to alter its collision course.

It's not Hope that will eradicate poverty, disease, cruelty and ignorance, and it's not hope that brings a child out of earthquake rubble: it's determined effort by desperate people.

Maybe Hope limps along behind, giving them the occasional prod, and that's fair enough. Homer was groping his way towards understanding this when he wrote the Iliad. 'Strength is felt from hope, and from despair,' he said. He got it the wrong way round, of course, but at least he acknowledged that despair plays a part in being strong and successful in life.

But if the ancient Greeks were aware of the power of despair three thousand years ago, how come its role has been subverted by the lesser construct of hope?

The short answer is that western society has been seduced by ruthless leaders, religious and secular alike, whose objective is to keep us all in a state of compliant catalepsy. They *want* us to hope that they will provide better government than their predecessors; to hope that things will be better in the next life than they are in this; to hope that taxes will be reduced; to hope that education and health will be improved … that public utilities will all work together in the same hole in the road, at night, not in the rush hour.

If we swallow their garbage, they'll carry on conning us and ensuring that they, not us, rule this 'democratic' roost. But, as we saw with the poll tax, despair (in the form of public riot) wins, hands down!

As a civilisation poised on the brink of calamity and disaster, we can no longer afford the invidious luxuries of calm and hope, and in case you have any lingering doubts, read on.

A brief history of despair

I recently quoted from the Iliad. This was not to show what a polymath I am, what a well read chap, what a wide-ranging set of philosophical values I embrace: all this is true, but my main purpose was to illustrate a point by using references from other clever people, among whom Homer was merely a convenient starting point.

Take Jean Anouilh. I don't know who she was or how to pronounce her name, but in 1934 she wrote: 'You may not know it, but at the far end of despair, there is a white clearing where one is almost happy.'

You could argue with her lax use of parenthetical commas and with the fact that you don't know exactly what she means, but the gist is obvious.

Take Dostoevski, who wrote these words in 1864: 'In despair there are the most intense enjoyments, especially when one is very acutely conscious of the hopelessness of one's position.' Quite so! And there are prescient echoes in his use of the impersonal third-person-singular to Her Majesty the Queen's recent reference to her *anus horibbilis* (*sic*).

Then again, in 1854 an economist called Thoreau said: 'The mass of men lead lives of quiet resignation. What is called resignation is confirmed desperation. From the desperate city you go into the desperate country, and have to console yourself with the bravery of minks and muskrats ...'

(*Professor.* Please forgive my on-line interruption, but I have been thinking that perhaps your readers will become as baffled as myself with regards to the line of advancement of your thinking at this point. Perhaps you would achieve more readership bonding if you were to quote the Vedic sages, of whose work I am a most profound advocate, rather than a random selection of dubious luminaries. Yours affectionately and slightly discomfortably. *Editor-Designate Rambal Phal.*)

(*Phal.* Damn you, Phal! How did you do that? *AC.*)

(*Professor.* With a certain degree of ingenuity and a Master's degree in computer algorithms and hacking protocols, in addition to which I have been making electricity to power this transmission through the small methane gas cell that I have inserted into the anus of my donkey. Indeed it was your recent reference to Her Majesty the Queen's

Latin quotation that promoted me to make this transmission. But do you not think I am making a valid point? *Editor-Designate Rambal Phal.*)

(*Phal.* Consider any implied contract with me terminated with immediate effect. *AC.*)

(*Professor.* I am laughing most hysterically at your wit and wisdom, for we do not as yet have a contract with which I can be terminated. Even so, I will insert into your work a Word 7 file containing a list of ancient Vedic sayings regarding the subject of despair. *Editor-Designate Rambal Phal.*)

_____

(*Pub.* This lunatic Phal has somehow managed to hack into my system. He is threatening to download some of his rubbish into my book. *AC.*)

(*Arnie.* Not much I can do about that, I'm afraid. The thought strikes me that such an addition could increase the value of the manuscript from an acquisitive university library's point of view. *Pub.*)

_____

The physiology of despair

No book about despair would be complete without an incursion into its physiology, and we begin with the physical symptoms. At first sight, these resemble those of panic, such as shortness of breath, popping eyes, clenched fists, etc. However, there is a small but significant difference: whereas panic is and always will be an end in itself, despair is a means to an end.

And Mother Nature has made allowances for this. She knows that despair almost always ends in a supreme effort to surmount apparently insurmountable odds, and she has equipped each of us to recognise such a difference as She does.

The mechanism for this activity is a section of the hypothalamus, a gland situated a small distance away from the pituitary gland and in close association with it. Called the *medial glandusa coptus*, this vital piece of human anatomy is provoked into action by any situation requiring desperate measures.

In the first phase of action, a cocktail of hormones is released by the hypothalamus into the lymphatic system. This transports the mixture to the pituitary gland, and during this journey various secondary activities take place, as α-adrenaline reacts with β-mustaphone which is released by instructions from the cortico-sterex section of the brain.

This kick-starts even more neuro-lymphatic reactions involving other endocrine glands and one or two exocrines as well.

As a result of all this natural activity, massive amounts of potassium ions flood through the relevant synaptic gateways, producing highly focused muscle reactions.

Research in my independent laboratories has confirmed that this procedure can temporarily multiply the normal strength of a human muscle by a factor of up to fifty, thus accounting for the phenomenal acts of courage, strength and heroism recounted in the following pages.

———————————

(Oh no! Talking of human muscles, the lumpen mass of them that constitutes the UK postal service in this remote and mountainous area is negotiating his way past the ribbon wire towards my front door, even as I write ...)

———————————

Professor A. Claggerhaus Esq
c/o Bewildered Books
Ceredigion, Wales

Dear Professor Claggerhaus

Most sincere thanks for your generous and whimsical acceptance of my application and to your jesting on-line comment regarding my contract.

Do not worry about my travelling expenses. My village has no airport, and therefore I will be obliged to journey to London by alternative modes of transportation, keeping you in almost daily touch via a system of postcards.

When I am arriving, perhaps we can come to a gentleman's arrangement with regard to the savings I will have been making on your travelling expenses budget; let us say, on a fifty to fifty basis, in addition to my salary.

You may be delighted to know that much of the journeying will of necessity be taking place from the back of a donkey, but such are the wondrous vicissitudes of modern technology that the route I am proposing to take remains within the Global Positioning System of geo-stationary satellites.

The conclusion of this is that I will know exactly where I am to within five metres at any time of the day or night. I am thus sure to be able to find your return address, even though you seem to have obliterated it by accident from your letter to me.

I am remaining, Sir, In deepest Gratitude

Dr. Rambal Phal (Twice removed from the well known curry)

PS Could you kindly forward to me by irrevocable bankers draft my first three months of salary, care of the District Sub-Post Office, Ashikaga?

PPS I am eager to present my forthcoming consort with a suitable gift of Ann Summers underwear and consequently am very desirous of knowing the size of her mammalian appendages to the nearest Imperial measurement.

PPPS With regard to Vedic sayings, I am still wondering how to create the appropriate zipped file to send across to you via novel data compression technology algorithms. But do not worry. It is merely a matter of time.

———————————

(*Arnie*: I received the copy of Dr Phal's letter this morning. I agree: he is either the most persistent hoaxer in the world or a raving lunatic. Either way, there is not much I can do about it, as I am currently engaged in negotiating a contract with the University of Maryland's Archive of Creative Writing Drivel. Were the stains on the copy of Dr Phal's letter tears or coffee? Not that it matters. Great stuff! Just keep it coming. *Pub.*)

Case studies

Even the most rigorous researcher into human behaviour must rely from time to time on empirical or anecdotal evidence to support a conjecture or hypothesis. In the matter of despair versus hope as the prime motivator in dealing with the troubles of life, there is no shortage of such material.

After a lifetime of such research, I can state with certainty that despair leads to achievement while hope leads to disappointment. Despair is the incentive that can drive people to superhuman effort. Hope is the last refuge of the weak-minded.

Contrast the person who is awakened by a nocturnal fight between a neighbouring married couple and says, 'I do hope Mrs So-and-so will be all right', with the one who says, 'I'm going next door to sort it out!' Surely the reaction of such a desperately sleepless person is more positive and effective than that of a wishy-washy hopeful person.

In over thirty years of intense study, I have managed to find only one circumstance where hope was responsible for a desired result. Schooled, as I am, in the academic rigour of a

balanced argument, I present it as the
exception that proves the rule. It happened in
the operating theatre of a well known
orthopaedic hospital in the West Midlands.

Case 1 – The philosophical comedian

A certain Mr Jonathan Middlehew was
renowned for his act as 'Jonathan Middlehew –
The Philosophical Comedian' on Saturday
evenings in the local pub. Following a less than
philosophical argument with a drunken husband
(who objected to Mr Middlehew picking on his
wife to ask her Socratic-style questions such as,
'Tell us, my dear, does your husband give it to
you on a regular or irregular basis, and how
would you define regular?'), Middlehew was
scheduled to have his severely damaged left leg
amputated above the knee. He was given his
pre-op sedatives and received a general
anaesthetic.

It so happened that Mr Middlehew was one of
those unfortunate people who are resistant to
anaesthetics, and he was both conscious and
alert as the surgeon began drawing his blue lines
in preparation for the first incision.

'I hope you've got the right leg there, doctor,'
he said jocularly. 'Or do I mean the left leg? In

fact, is the left leg the right leg, or vice versa?'

The surgeon was so confused by this that he decided to check the case notes. He discovered that he had, in fact, drawn his blue lines on the wrong leg, which was the right leg. And all because of his patient's expression of hope.

Perhaps there are other cases in world history where hope has triumphed over adversity, but I doubt it. In my experience, despair invariably wins the day, as in the following examples selected at random from my exhaustive compilation of cases in which desperation has led to acts of heroism, sacrifice and supreme effort.

Case 2 – the pet dog

At approximately 4:15pm on 16 June 1903, Mr Henry Walstead of Highbury Avenue, St Albans, a one-armed man with colonic hernia, was walking his dog Aristotle past council road works when a cat ran into the unfinished trench. The dog broke free from Mr Walstead's restraining leash and followed the cat into the trench, which collapsed on top of it. During the next half hour, Mr Walstead single-handedly scraped an estimated fourteen tons of soil and builder's debris in order to free his pet. When interviewed by a local journalist he said: 'For the first few minutes I hoped Aristotle would manage to dig himself free, but as time ticked away and his barks became weaker and weaker I became desperate …'

Case 3 – the winning try

During the final moments of the Pontypridd versus Llanelli rugby match at home in Llanelli in November 1854, the visitors were two clear points in the lead and about to score yet another try, when Dai Roberts the Llanelli scrum-half caught sight of his six-year-old son looking at him from the side line.

'His two eyes were boring holes in me,' Roberts said later. 'I knew that if I failed him now, my life as his father would be purposeless. The situation was desperate, for the club and for my family.'

The Pontypridd forwards surged forward in what they anticipated would be the concluding and decisive try of the match. Their scrum half flicked the ball to the quarter-backs. And, with a gigantic leap across the scrum, Roberts intercepted it!

As he began his run for the opponents' try line, first one, then two, then all eight forwards leapt on him, expecting him to crash to his knees, but the desperate Roberts managed to stay on his feet, plunging towards the halfway line, then the ten-yard line, then the twenty-two-yard line.

The opposing backs threw themselves onto the frenzied mass of Pontypridd players, but with a final gargantuan effort Roberts shook them off and sailed through the air to place the ball neatly between the goal posts for a brilliant try and an easy conversion.

His achievement was all the more remarkable when, after a subsequent visit to his doctor, it was discovered that he had suffered three crushed vertebrae, a broken thumb and a blister on his left heel.

'All in a day's work for a miner,' he said modestly. 'Mind you, I wouldn't have been able to look my son in the face if we'd lost to Pontypridd.'

———————————

(*Pub*. Oh God! I can hear the modem clicking. It's probably Phal. He's …)

———————————

Sayings of the Vedic sages extracted from the original by Dr Rambal Phal for his employer-designate Professor Arnie Claggerhaus

Saying No. 1

Happy is he who is desperate, for he knows the true happiness of desperation.

Saying No. 2

When your brother tells you to despair not, then truly it is said that you should despair.

Saying No. 3

This Saying is not true.

Saying No. 4

Life is like a rainbow.

Saying No. 5

I say, I say, I say. What is the difference between Max Miller and a lady tossing herself off a cliff?

<u>Saying No. 6</u>

WINWORD HAS CAUSED A FATAL EXCEPTION
ERROR IN MODULE 0087 334H 5TL9 AT
LOCATION 0F01 1RH4 229P.

MR GATES APOLOGISES FOR THIS
DISRUPTION TO YOUR WORK AND ACCEPTS
FULL RESPONSIBILITY.

SEND YOUR REQUEST FOR COMPENSATION
DIRECT TO HIM VIA:
BILL.GATES@WWW.MICROSOFT.COM/CRASH-
TEAM/POLITE-RESPONSE-INFINITE-LOOP-
TEAM/TRASH-BIN.HML

(*Phal.* You crashed my computer, you utter moron.
It's taken me ages to reboot. *AC.*)

(*Professor.* Utmost apologies. My donkey
managed to scavenge an over-ripe mango, thus
resulting in a temporary but highly peaked voltage
overload. I am keeping him hobbled, so this
should not be happening again. *Editor-Designate
Rambal Phal. Dr.*)

(*Phal.* Damn right, it won't. I'm disabling my
modem. Stuff that into your Global Positioning
System! What's more, I am going to write to my
ex-editor offering him his job back. *AC.*)

Paul Wilson

Author: The Little Book of Hope

c/o Penguin Books, London

Dear Mr Wilson

I am writing to you (a) on the assumption that I was correct in identifying you as the erstwhile editor of my current writing project, The Slightly Larger Book of Despair and (b) in the desperation that, if assumption (a) is correct, you will not yet have been offered new employment.

There is nothing you could do to edit my new book that would be worse than that which seems about to happen to it. It would be difficult to explain, but trust me.

Please, please come back.

Yours in desperation

Arnie Claggerhaus (Prof.)

PS I should make it clear that your salary will not be paid during the period beginning on the day I sacked you and the day on which you may or may not take up your new re-appointment. The same is true for holiday entitlement and pension.

PPS I would appreciate an apology for your 'pompous pommy bastard' jibe. A chap has his reputation to think of.

Case 4 – The frozen climbers

During a snow storm in the Trossach Mountains in Scotland, 45-year-old mountaineer Ross McBride slipped on a patch of ice and slid a hundred feet into a crevasse. His partner Wally Simpson managed to halt his fall, and Mr McBride spent the night dangling at the end of the rope. Mr Simpson, meanwhile, was wrestling with his conscience. Unable to pull on the rope with his frozen hands, he knew that if he continued supporting his friend, they would both die of exposure.

'At the end of the day,' he told reporters, 'I knew it was either Ross or me. I was preparing to cut the rope with my *skean dhu*, but fortunately I remembered that Ross owed me a fiver, so I pulled the bastard back up and made him hand it over. Frankly, I'd given up all hope of ever seeing the money again, and a good job too, otherwise this might never have happened.'

(*Pub.* U-oh! Here comes the postman again. He's waving a postcard. Can't you do <u>anything</u>? *Arnie.*)

(*Arnie.* Sorry. Your email arrived just as I was popping out to Oddbins. *Pub.*)

Professor A. Claggerhaus Esq
c/o Bewildered Books
Ceredigion, Wales

Dear Professor Claggerhaus

Munich is a fine city of much architectural merit but with few facilities for my donkey other than a comprehensive and accurate system of fining-on-the-spot for audacious deposits. In vain do I wring my hands and protest, but the evidence is carried to Court in sealed bags and exacerbated by the electrocution of a city veterinary agent who carelessly attempted to extract the terminal wires of my generating set from the animal in question. The entire business is delaying the continuing phase of my journey to you, but please not to despair (no pun being intended). I am arriving in Ceredigion via several other places within the next few weeks.

I am,
amicably yours
despite official setbacks
Dr Rambal Phal

———————————

(*Arnie*. Phal's Munich postcard was grrreat! I'm into five figures and counting. What a shame we cannot contact Dr Phal and ask him to extend his journey so as to take in Rekjavik. That <u>would</u> be a scoop! *Pub.*)

(*Pub.* It is difficult for me to put into words how I feel about your constant striving for commercial success. Frankly, it appalls me, and I intend to concentrate on the book which, in case you have forgotten, is the actual point of this exercise. *Arnie.*)

Case 5 – The pregnant motorist

At 4:30pm on Wednesday 15 June 1999, Mrs Dorothy Skelmersdale was driving herself to the maternity unit of St Olaf's Hospital in Pengary when a 40-tonne articulated lorry lost a tyre, crossed the central reservation of the M47 motorway, skidded across three fields of turnips, overturned onto Mrs Skelmersdale's Mini and also trapped Mr Bert Wishbone, an old-age pensioner who was out for a walk with his Zimmer frame.

While the lorry driver remained asleep at the wheel, Mr Wishbone lifted the vehicle with one hand and delivered Mrs Skelmersdale's baby with the other. By the time emergency services had arrived, he had bitten through the umbilical chord, cleaned up the afterbirth, licked the child clean, positioned it against its mother's breast, and given the lorry driver a bollocking.

Asked by reporters how he had managed such an amazing feat, Mr Wishbone said: 'I keep myself fit, don't I?'

He then collapsed and died. Post-mortem results showed a massive increase in the amount of potassium ions in his bloodstream, irrefutable proof that this modest man had acted heroically through desperation.

Telephone transcript #1

Source: BT Police Liaison Unit

Subscriber identified as: Professor Arnie Claggerhaus

BT Overseas Operator: Is that Professor Arnie Claggerhaus.

Subscriber: Yes.

BT Overseas Operator: Will you accept a reverse charge call from a Dr Rambal Phal speaking from a call box in …

Subscriber: No.

Call terminated by subscriber.

Case 6 – The heroic soldier

During WW1, Private Dennis Yardley experienced severe stomach cramps followed by a violent attack of diarrhoea. He reported to the medical tent and was prescribed a dose of arrowroot. An inexperienced orderly opened the wrong container and served Private Yardley with an 8 ounce dose of quick-setting cement.

The following afternoon, when the whistles blew to commence the next offensive, Private Yardley informed his sergeant of his urgent need to evacuate his bowels.

'Well, well, well,' the sergeant is reported to have replied. 'Is that a fact?'

'It certainly is, sergeant,' replied Private Yardley. 'I am truly desperate!'

'In that case, lad, you'll have to crap in Jerry's trenches, because our latrine bucket took a direct hit from a sniper's bullet.'

As the officers blew their whistles to launch the next wave of infantry, Private Yardley was first over the top. He stormed across five hundred yards of barbed wire, mines, grenades and withering cross-fire from hundreds of water-cooled Maxim machine guns, entered the German trenches, and killed the enemy commander with a single evacuation of his bowels.

In all, 456 German soldiers were overcome with fumes, and a further 1567 surrendered.

Private Yardley was posthumously awarded thirty-five Victoria Crosses, a record that has yet to be beaten by any serving soldier, sailor or airman.

Case 7 – How desperation enabled a 32-year-old brick-layer to perform micro-surgery on his mate's severed legs using commonly available building materials ...

_____

(Aieee! Is there no respite? Here's that dratted postman. **Note to my Do List**: Remember to instruct the sorting office to re-direct all mail with overseas postage stamps back to the sender. With luck, this will put an end to Phal's constant harrassment.)

_____

Professor A. Claggerhaus Esq
c/o Bewildered Books
Ceredigion, Wales

Dear Professor Claggerhaus
Ah! Gay Paris! No exaggeration can be made of
her manifold delights by so humble a traveller as
mygoodself, not least being the apparent inability
of her citizens to notice the deposition of asinine by-
products. This is due, no doubt of it, to the all-
pervading perfumes of beautiful ladies. Indeed, my
donkey has captured the hearts of all-and-sundry
and especially in a jazz club where his capacity for
electrical generation over-came a power failure within
the amplification system, thus enabling the
continuance of the evening performances. The jazz
club owner is promising us bed-and-breakfast and
transportation to Amsterdam in return for what he
is calling a late night private party of like-minded
animal lovers and photographers.
    I am,
    remaining
    your
    imminent editor,
    Dr Rambal Phal

_____

(I must ignore this lunacy and finish my book.)

Make use of your despair

Many of my clients ask me: 'Okay, so you tell me that despair can help me to overcome irresistible obstacles and to perform extraordinary feats of accomplishment, acts of bravery and heroism under extreme conditions – can I tap into this potential at will, or do I have to wait for a random incident to produce the required results?'

As with all such deeply probing questions, there is no straightforward answer. The un-straightforward answer is: Yes and Yes; Yes and No, No and Yes, and No and No, depending on the circumstances.

In the ideal case, you will absorb the wisdom in this slightly larger book and reach the level of understanding that allows me to answer: Yes and No. The following procedure is designed to accomplish this for you.

Our objective is to induce in ourselves such an absolute state of despair at all times of the day and night that we generate vast amounts of potassium ions to hold in reserve and release at will, thus providing super-human strength on demand.

We have to reach such a nadir in our psyche that every nerve and muscle fibre is directed towards what I call the Great Jump Upwards. A useful example is provided by Olympic pole vaulting.

Let us assume that you are rated tenth in the world and that not even your closest family or best friends expect you to reach the finals and certainly not to gain a medal if you do. The very last thing you must do is to enlist their support in the difficult task ahead, because this will merely confirm the failure that everyone expects you to experience.

Your first task is to alienate them! There are four key steps involved:

- Withdraw from all co-operative activities in the home and at work
- Reject all advice, guidance and sympathy
- Boast that no one else stands a chance
- Eat lots of garlic and bananas

A rigorous application of the first three techniques will quickly destroy all your relationships, leaving you a pariah in your community and among your fellow sportsmen. The garlic exuded by your body will enhance this separation, and the bananas are the source of the potassium you will need to boost your performance to podium standards.

As you stand with your pole at the ready, you will feel the palpable scorn, derision, and hatred of those who formerly loved, admired and respected you, and you will begin your metamorphosis from caterpillar to ravening butterfly. Your hypothalamus will release its potent charge of steroids, seratonins, pheromones and nucleic acids. Your pituitary will pump alpha block busters into your blood stream. And massive, unstoppable quantities of potassium ions will trigger every muscle in your body to world-record-breaking heights of achievement.

It is important to reinforce this procedure after every successful vault by making rude and conceited gestures to the audience and fellow competitors. As the hatred and disgust grows, so also will your desperate efforts to do the one thing that will put them all firmly in their places. You will win!

I realise that not everybody wants to gain an Olympic gold medal for pole vaulting, but the withdraw-reject-boast-eat-garlic-and-bananas procedure can be adapted to almost all human situations.

In addition to such specifically targeted objectives, you must generate a supportive environment for your desperate efforts. The first and arguably the most important involves negative financial management.

- Use all your credit cards to the limit
- Borrow from every financial institution that invites you to do so and spend the money on valueless goods and services
- Use hire purchase and leasing arrangements to acquire everything you've ever wanted

As the final demands roll in, your desperation level will rise like the Limpopo River. Then, just as it seems that things could not get worse, indulge in a little light crime. Shoplifting is good, because you can stay out of prison for longer periods. If, however, you seek an accelerated path to utter desperation, you might consider a bit of grievous bodily harm and an outburst in Court. **On no account should you indulge in excessive drinking or the taking of drugs!**

Alcohol and drugs do the one thing that will defeat your purpose: they destroy potassium ions, turning them into combined radicals that will clog up the synaptic pathways to success.

If you apply yourself assiduously to this

technique, it becomes progressively easier to achieve your objectives. Ultimately, you will exist in a constant state of absolute despair, ready to explode into action, a bit like anger does for the Incredible Hulk ...

(Arrrrrgh!!!! The Postman!!!!!!!! Please, *please* let him not deliver another postcard. I couldn't bear it, I really couldn't. It's not as if he chooses nice pictures. It's always half a dozen views across the bay or a new shopping mall. He brings a new and deeper meaning to the word naff.)

Professor A. Claggerhaus Esq
c/o Bewildered Books
Ceredigion, Wales

Dear Professor Claggerhaus
Gosh and golly! I am almost falling for the
blandishments of evil men and women whose
looseness of moral behaviour is knowing few bounds.
My poor donkey is currently recovering from an
over-abundance of attentions which a natural
reluctance and a shortage of the appropriate words
prevents me from describing. Suffice it to say that
I am writing this in the back of a container lorry
on a North Sea ferry which we are sharing with a
group of colourfully but poorly clad people whose
sole pastime appears to be the surreptitious
extraction of items from purses and pockets. Into
what I am getting myself into now, I exclaim!
    I am,
    regrettably
    cut short by an attack of marine nausea
    Dr Rambal Phal

───────────────

(Phal's nausea is the best news I've had all week;
on the other hand, his presence on a ferry brings
great foreboding and despair. What am I to make
of all this?)

Ten Golden Rules

Having introduced you to some of the great benefits of despair and to the general method of achieving a state of desperation, I now list my Ten Golden Rules of Despair for you to follow to assist you in your search for perfect desperation.

Each and every one of them will increase your chances of success, partly by expunging all attempts to remain calm, serene and hopeful and partly by confusing you as to the purpose in your life (see later); in fact, the more you apply the Rules, the less purpose there will seem to be, and the more unsure of yourself you will become.

- Set yourself impossible goals
- Avoid sunshine, positive people and optimists
- Take laxatives before every important event in your life
- Write a list of essential dos and don'ts and then reverse it
- If anyone begins to rely on you, let them down badly
- Seek the company of losers
- Turn vegan and eat plenty of museli

- Read Hansard each day
- Refuse to cooperate with authority
- Carry a plentiful supply of ashes, and wear sackcloth

Remember, though, that these are my Rules. You may wish to adapt them to your own circumstances or to increase them.

(One of my students recently pointed out that having ten of anything is relatively easy to remember. She advocates having Twenty-three Golden Rules of Despair. Not only are twenty-three things harder to remember than ten things, but the number itself is unremarkable and therefore more difficult to remember than ten. Every time she tries to remember her Twenty-three Golden Rules, she becomes increasingly desperate, as the minutes slip away. So hopeless is her plight that she plans to increase the number of her Rules to One-Hundred-and-Seventeen, which gives her the added problem of conjuring up enough relevant aphorisms to complete the list.)

Telephone transcript #2
Source: BT/Police Liaison Unit
Caller ID: J. Wilson
Subscriber ID: Professor A. Claggerhaus

Wilson: Hi, Arnie. How are things?
Claggerhaus: Don't ask.
Wilson: You're sounding a bit down in the dumps. What's the matter?
Claggerhaus: Down in the dumps? I should say I'm down in the dumps. So would you be down in the dumps if you had an incessant bombardment of emails and postcards from a raving lunatic who claims to be riding a donkey over to my place from his village in the mid-Asian plateau.
Wilson: You really mustn't worry. It's giving us a unique annotated manuscript sales opportunity. If things are getting on top of you, I dare say we could extend the copy-date. You know. Give you a chance to relax for a few days …
Claggerhaus: It's no good. I disabled my modem, but he's trying to get to me with reverse charge phone calls. You hear all these clicks on the line? I wouldn't be surprised if the bastard was bugging me. I'm at my wits end. I have to inhale pure oxygen twice every hour.
Wilson: Is that why you haven't been replying to my emails?
Claggerhaus: What emails?
Wilson: There you are, you see. Why not re-boot and filter out his stuff?

Claggerhaus: It's all very well for you. You sit there at your big desk, with your big cigar clamped in your big mouth, living off the efforts of people like me who are in at the sharp end …

Wilson: I don't smoke cigars.

Claggerhaus: What's that got to do with it? Everything else is true.

Wilson: What's all that clicking on the line?

Claggerhaus: I told you. I'm being bugged. If this gets any worse, I'll be back in an iron lung before you can say emphysema.

Wilson: I can't even spell it, never mind say it. Look, Arnie, I have to go. Take a week off from Ceredigion. Go to Kent. Travel on the Romney-to-Hythe miniature railway. Sketch the gravestones in Lydd churchyard. But for Christ's sake, snap out if it, will you?

Claggerhaus: I'm trying, I really am. It's not easy. I'm going to nail my letter box shut tomorrow.

Wilson: Sounds good, sounds good. Look, I'll call you next Monday, okay? Keep up the good work.

Claggerhaus: What's the point, that's what I'd like to know?

Call terminated by subscriber.

Living testimony

At this point, I was planning to convey to you some verbatim reports of people suffering from the deepest despair, but my publisher remains insistent that my work contains all the associated editorial notes, amendments and background required by the university library with which he is currently negotiating. As a result, my own, personal experience in writing this book transcends the third party material that I was proposing to include in this chapter.

To begin with, I am no longer sure what I am supposed to be doing or where I am supposed to be going. Until now, I have been accorded the respect of the eminent academician, the revered consultant … I was allowed to conduct my research and record its progress and achievements in peace and quiet, but now I have to put up with constant interruption from my publisher, the telephone and the postman.

And what on earth am I to do about the abominable and remorselessly cheerful Dr Rambal Phal?

There is something of a mystery about him. For one thing, how did he manage to see my advertisement in the Evening Standard on the day of publication when he lives in a village in either India or Pakistan without telephone, newsagent or airport?

Then again, is it credible that the anal fuel cell in his asinine companion is sufficient to power the amplifier of his global positioning system?

What a dilemma! I cannot sack him because I have not appointed him. And I cannot prevent him from making his journey because I cannot communicate with him.

As I write I can see the postman's little red van ricocheting its way down the mountain road with the morning's delivery. I try to cheer myself with the thought that he is merely bringing final demands for council tax and threatening letters from the Inland Revenue, but the moment recedes as he extricates himself from his damnable vehicle waving yet another postcard from Phal ...

Horrors! I can see the picture from here. An architect's impression of the third draft of the new Welsh Assembly building in Cardiff. Or is it Swansea?

His message is that he and his donkey will arrive within five metres of my front door at precisely four o'clock this afternoon.

A desperate journey

As you might imagine, Dr Phal's most recent postcard filled me with despair, and I returned to the writing of my book, my body surging with potassium ions and renewed vigour. However, the time of his scheduled arrival came and went, and by five o'clock that afternoon I succumbed to an attack of hope that left me seriously incapacitated. At six o'clock, however, Dr Phal and his donkey arrived, having momentarily lost touch with the international global positioning system in the Talbot Hotel.

On seeing my plight, Dr Phal suggested I accompany him to his home (which turns out to be not in India or Pakistan but in Nepal) in order to finish my book in peace and quiet. When I objected that the cost would be too great he smiled and said he would take care of it. And so he did.

Among his innumerable academic qualifications is a Master's degree in grant applications for charitable ventures. In less than a week he had gained pledges of several million dollars from more than 300 companies and organisations for a sponsored walk from

Tregaron to Nepal, comprising himself as fund-raiser and GPS navigator, the anally electrified donkey as transport, and myself as the focus of the venture, complete with miniaturised respirator and life support system powered by the donkey's flatulence.

In vain did I try to protest, but each attempt to do so resulted in a facial rictus that all the do-gooders interpreted as a willing smile.

And so we began our journey, of which the least said the better. I cannot resist, however, a reference to Amsterdam, where Dr Phal said he had to repay a debt of honour involving the donkey. All well and good, but for over an hour I was left without life support as a succession of free-thinkers cavorted with the donkey.

When I at last managed to reach a wall socket and stick my wires inside, I was momentarily turned into a cable TV set, possibly the most disturbing experience I have ever suffered at my own hands.

As the insane journey continued, I lost count of the days, the weeks, the months ... Towards the end, I passed into a strange limbo. I forgot what I was supposed to be doing. I forgot where I was going. I almost forgot who I was.

And then, one day, Dr Phal bent over me and

said, 'We have arrived. Now we can begin to determine the truth.'

Arrived where? Truth about what?

I peered through my respirator goggles, but all I could see was a dense, all pervading whiteness. But I knew it must be somewhere extremely cold because hoar-frost was forming on the lenses. Could this be Nepal?

Indeed it could!

The ashram in the sky

Okay, so my ashram is not exactly in the sky, but 18,000 feet up the Himalayas is near enough for me. It's not really an ashram either; merely a two-man-one-donkey survival tent from Millets, with a space for rucksacks and electrical equipment. But you take what you can get in these parts.

I cannot tell you how my life has changed, here, with my companion Dr Rambal Phal and his donkey for company. We have everything we need for the good life, including a constant supply of ice and electricity from the donkey's anal methane-to-DC converter and an old mercury arc rectifier to convert the 12 volts DC to 230 volts AC for my respirator which we found in a glacier (the rectifier, not the respirator); refuse, no doubt, from an erstwhile attempt by other emphysemics on the summit of Everest, which is not far away.

Having so much time to contemplate, I see now that my true purpose was always to find this place. Here I have been able to develop my work for the fulfilment of mankind's most challenging aspirational desires.

In my case, this has resulted in a severe attack of the new mental disease to which I referred earlier in this manuscript: phobiophobia. It combines the symptoms of panic attacks, hysteria, catatonia, narcolepsy, photophobia, agoraphobia, claustrophobia, others too dreadful to think about, and others for which no word has yet been invented, such as the fear of unlimited hordes of disciples finding their way from Wales and seeking my leadership.

Interruption and encumbrance

Do not misunderstand me about disciples. Under normal circumstances they would be most welcome, but I am here for one reason, and one alone – to concentrate on my work, free from interruption and encumbrance.

Dr Rambal is an inspiration in this respect. His unflagging optimism, cheerfulness and good humour are the source of constant despair to me. If I were able to move my frozen arms and legs I would undoubtedly have killed him by now.

Meanwhile, with cryogenic gangrene affecting most of my extremities, I am reduced to dictating my book to him, in the certain knowledge that he is editing it beyond all recognition in order to increase its value in the world market for annotated manuscripts.

Well, that's the good news.

The bad news

The bad news is, we are running out of forage for the donkey, and the light is beginning to flicker and fail. I asked Dr Phal what his know-all Vedic sages would do in such circumstances. He gave me his most brilliant smile and said:

'They would die, Professor Claggerhaus, they would die.'

Determined that he should not have the final word on the matter I asked if he recalled the Vedic sayings that had caused my computer to crash, and in particular Saying No. 5.

'Most assuredly,' he beamed. 'Life is like a rainbow, is it not?'

Summoning my final and most desperate effort, I raised myself as best I could and looked him full in his shining, optimistic little face.

'No, Dr Phal, it is not. And, what's more, your Max Miller quotation in Saying No. 6 is a corruption of the original. The correct version is that a mountaineer on a narrow ledge meets an attractive young lady coming the other way, and he does not know whether to block her passage or toss himself off.'

I would like to think that as the light vanishes I detected a look of utter dismay on his features. It might have been a shadow, but then he said plaintively, 'You never did conclude my contact with the ex-Miss World contestant; and neither did you supply me with her mammalian measurements in Imperial units.'

As I lie in the cold, velvety blackness, I rejoice: I have, at last, discovered a crack in the good Doctor's previously impenetrable coating of insane optimism.

Immortality: the greatest triumph of despair?

I have been keeping a secret from Dr Phal. While he takes notes on my behalf for the conclusion of my book, I have secretly been warming my fingers by placing them into the donkey's anus, a survival technique taught to me by an SAS friend. This has enabled me to write these final and very personal notes in private and sew them into the lining of my wallet so that my publisher can add them to the book after Dr Phal's final annotations.

A philosopher and *personnage extraordinaire* such as myself often finds himself (and occasionally herself) faced with a sensitive issue, a factor that cannot be left from an argument despite the fact that it might cause offence; indeed, it is the mark of a great intellect and leader that he (and infrequently she) will vouchsafe a notion that can topple civilisations.

I see now that my journey on the back of a donkey to these fabled mountains was pre-ordained, a present-day pilgrimage that parallels that of other holy men, and I have come to the conclusion that, if monumental despair triggers ordinary humans to perform superhuman acts of courage and strength, then infinite despair is a prelude to ever-lasting life.

Incredible? Outlandish? Far fetched?

Maybe so. But before I present you with my revolutionary hypothesis on the role of desperation in the divinity of Jesus Christ, allow me in my last mortal moments to refer to the Gaia theory of the Earth Mother's role in the continuance of Life and the modern world's consequential attack of politically correct feminism, whose adherents claim that Life is propagated by the female of the species, with the male reduced to a momentary fumble in the haystacks.

Nonsense

Let me ask those who espouse such nonsense a single question: do eggs wriggle in the ovaries?

Of course they don't! It's the spermatozoa that do the wriggling. To paraphrase one of my most distinguished predecessors: I wriggle, therefore I exist. It is clearly the male of the species who carries the gift of life from one generation to another. The female simply provides the transportation, so let's have no more of this female supremacy malarkey!

Darwin was wrong?

Faced with the distinct possibility that within a few moments of my faded existence I might discover that the Popes and the Archbishops have been right and that Darwin was wrong, I now introduce to you the world-shattering notion that Jesus Christ Himself was aware of the awesome power of despair and that He, like me, was not above using it for His own ends.

When those nails were being hammered in and He was left hanging on the cross in terrible pain, do we hear Him saying to the centurions: 'I hope this will be okay; I have a resurrection to do in three days time'?

No! His last words as an as-yet-unresurrected being were to ask His Father why he had been forsaken. In other words, He had reached an absolute nadir, and, as we are told that He did everything for a purpose, it can be argued that had He not despaired during the crucifixion as the gospels inform us, He would not have accomplished the resurrection and the consequent ascension would have proved impossible to undertake.

If final proof be needed: in my own blackest hour of desperation and facing my own approaching demise, I am experiencing a strange light-headedness. And my blackest moment of despair has attacked me when, in a moment of weakness, I find myself hoping that my own resurrection will not take the full three days. It's sixty degrees below freezing up here, and, in the background, I can hear Dr Phal murmuring: 'The Arabs say that Life is like a cucumber'.

Publisher's statement

Alongside the manuscript of Professor Claggerhaus's book, the rescue team discovered his Last Will and Testament in which he leaves his body to the Bronglais Hospital in Aberystwyth on condition that they count his potassium ions and publish the results on the Internet. However, his body remained undiscovered.

Dr Rambal Phal, his constant colleague during his final, desperate months, saved the manuscript and returned to the University of Darjeeling where he is currently engaged on a new doctoral thesis entitled *Viviophobia – the morbid fear of being alive: a case study from Ceredigion and Nepal.*

Meanwhile, a rumour is circulating among those among who such rumours circulate that senior figures in the UK security services are speculating that the disappearance of Professor Claggerhaus is the culmination of an elaborate plan to avoid his paranoid feelings of being under surveillance. His file is therefore being kept open, in case (quote) 'he re-emerges to threaten the security and peace of mind of the Nation, with his outlandish and seditious teachings and slighting references to the ethnicity of the British Monarchy' (unquote).

The two security file notes that follow were sent to me anonymously, with a request that I remit the sum of £5000 by electronic fund transfer to a numbered bank account in the Isle of Man, or else.

To preserve the editorial independence of Bewildered Books, I have not complied with this request.

TOP SECRET- 1

Reference: Claggerhaus A.

From: Field Operative PFU 34 aka Rambal Phal
c/o District Sub-Post Office
Ashikaga
Either India or Pakistan

To: MI5/Head of Section PFU

Not knowing what has befallen Professor Claggerhaus beyond the possibility that he is rolling from our tent and into an icy crevasse, I am rifling unsuccessfully through the items recovered from the ashram and discovering nothing except the manuscript of a book with which I was helping him and in which he appears to be advocating the use of despair as a means to triumph over adversity and to achieve everlasting life.

  In the absence of further information, I am prompted to enquire if this is for what we have been seeking?

  Please also inform me what are the letters PFU standing for in the acronyms of the Great British Intelligence Service, as my wife is desirous of boasting to our neighbours that I am secretly an undercover agent for the government of Her Majesty the Queen, c/o Buckingham Palace, London SW1.

TOP SECRET - 2

Reference: Claggerhaus A.

From: MI5/Head of Section PFU

To: Field Operative PFU 34 aka Rambal Phal
c/o District Sub-Post Office
Ashikaga
Either India or Pakistan

MI5 acronyms are explained to personnel on a strictly NTK basis. In the case of PFU personnel it is assumed that they do not need to know because they already work for the section and therefore such knowledge is no longer relevant. On the other hand, those who do not work for Section PFU may well fall into the NTK category.

Therefore, if you wish to pursue your enquiry further, you must follow the procedure outlined in Document PFU/NTK/4005/FU/BF. In brief, this means you must resign your current position as District Field Operative PFU 34 and re-apply on Form PFU/Recruitment/Asia/Ashikaga and District. At this stage, tick the Check Box on page 487 to indicate whether or not you wish to be considered eligible for a reassessment of your NTK status with regard to acronym MI5/268012/(PFU).

Please re-send your communication, as your previous communication has self-destructed and I have forgotten your first question.

The Claggerhaus trilogy

After a lifetime of trying to puzzle out why things are as they are and why people do the things they do, the founder of The Bewildered Publishing Company Ltd realised that he was in a constant state of bewilderment.

And so are most people he meets.

Particularly Professor Claggerhaus, who is currently working on the third and final book of his life trilogy:

'The Slightly Larger Book of Paranoia'

This will be followed by a range of Bewildered Book titles by other stupendous authors including but not necessarily in this order:

The Bewildered Motorist
The Bewildered Lover
The Bewildered Manager
The Bewildered Gardener
The Bewildered Cook
The Bewildered Philosopher
The Bewildered Golfer
The Bewildered Angler

If you have any good ideas about all this, or if you simply want to keep up with developments, visit our web page, email or fax us using the contact addresses on page 2. If you are <u>really</u> stuck, write to:

Bewildered Books
Argoed Hall
Tregaron
Ceredigion SY25 6JR
United Kindom

Printed by Cox & Wyman, Reading